What is Software Engineering?

G L Simons

PUBLISHED BY NCC PUBLICATIONS

British Library Cataloguing in Publication Data

Simons, G.L.
  What is software engineering?
  1. Electronic digital computers — Programming
  2. Computer engineering
  I. Title
  005.1'2   QA76.6

ISBN 0-85012-612-6

First published in 1987 by:
NCC Publications, The National Computing Centre Limited, Oxford Road, Manchester M1 7ED, England.

Typeset in Poppl Laudatio by Typeface Limited, Portland House, 103 Portland Street, Manchester M1 6DF and printed by Hobbs the Printers of Southampton.

ISBN 0-85012-612-6

Acknowledgement

I am grateful for the help of

Mike Wood (Manager, Presentation, STDC)

in the preparation of this publication. He discussed the project, read the text prior to printing, and made various useful suggestions and additions.

Geoff Simons
Chief Editor, NCC Publications

Contents

Page

Acknowledgement

Introduction   9

1   What is Software Engineering?   11

Introduction   11
Problems with Software   12
What is Software?   17
What is Engineering?   19
What is Software Engineering?   20
Aspects of the Life Cycle   25
The Relevance of Automation   30
    General   30
    Tools, Aids and Methods   31
Fourth-Generation Systems   32
Aims of Software Engineering   33

2 The Need for Software Engineering   35

Introduction   35
The Software Scene   36
The Software Crisis   37
Costs   40
Shortage of Specialists   42

Appendix

1 Where to Go for Help   45
2 Glossary   51
3 References and Bibliography   59

Introduction

Today increasing attention is being given to how software engineering can assist in the development of computer software. It is well known that software projects, as typically managed, stand a good chance of running over budgets and beyond timescales, and producing results that are disappointing. Software engineering is intended to help in this situation, to enable software purchasers and users to tackle the perceived software crisis.

There is widespread ignorance about the meaning of software engineering and the contribution it can make to the cost-effective development of good-quality software. The present book, the first output from a two-part project, describes simply and straightforwardly what software engineering is. It considers aspects of the software crisis and indicates where people can go for help and information. A glossary is included.

Later in 1987, *Introducing Software Engineering,* the second output from the project, will be published. By the same author of *What Is Software Engineering?,* it will provide a more detailed treatment of the ideas and techniques that are becoming essential to the development of adequate software within budgets and timescales.

1   What is Software Engineering?

INTRODUCTION

It is now impossible, in commerce and industry, to ignore the potential of computer-based systems. If companies and other organisations want to operate effectively in today's difficult environment they need to implement appropriate computer applications. But the computer is not a magic cure-all. The acquisition of computer equipment does not guarantee success in commercial enterprise or other types of activity. Users (and potential users) of computers need a systematic approach to the implementation and operation of computer-based facilities.

When a computer application is being planned or used, no aspect should be left to chance. Any ill-considered aspect – hardware, software, maintenance, security, staffing, etc – can incur unexpected costs and bring failure to an otherwise well planned system. Software, a main aspect of the present publication, is a vital feature of any modern computer system: if inadequate initial software is acquired, or subsequent application software is inefficiently developed, then at best the system will realise only part of its potential – and at worst it will run into catastrophic failure.

Today there is a growing body of attitudes, methods and tools designed to aid the development of software in a systematic way. It is increasingly feasible to *engineer* software cost-effectively to meet specific applications requirements. *Software engineering* – itself relying in part upon software tools – is evolving to cope with the various problems associated with the effective development of software. This chapter introduces the concept of software engineering by indicating:

— some current definitions and descriptions of software engineering;

— some of the phases and stages ('the life cycle') in software development that software engineering has to address;

— the relevance of automation to software engineering;

— the aims and impact of software engineering in the modern application of computer-based systems.

PROBLEMS WITH SOFTWARE

Many problems can arise in developing computer systems to perform tasks in the real world. Were the requirements fully understood? Clearly specified? Is the hardware powerful enough to cope with the range of intended applications? Will the software be reliable? Developed on time? Easy to maintain? Has due attention been given to the question of staffing (appointments, training, etc)? Such questions are often interrelated: for example, programmer productivity can determine whether software is developed on time.

It is also the case that ease in tackling *some* of the systems problems can lead to unrealistic optimism about implementation of the total system. For example, it is known that major problems are unlikely to arise with standard (non-innovative) hardware: the reliability and relative cheapness of digital electronic equipment can lead to false expectations about the speed and cost of implementing an effective system. In fact it has been found that most of the problems with large-scale computer projects relate to non-hardware issues; and that a major source of difficulty is software development. The larger the project, the larger the proportion of software development effort — and the greater the number and scale of the associated problems.

The software user — whether relying on in-house programming effort or obtaining software from external suppliers — is interested in software that does what is required and is easily maintainable. It is also essential that the software be delivered on time and within budget. In short, the user wants good quality software produced in an efficient cost-effective way. This does not seem an extravagant requirement, but problems can arise in many ways. The following quotations convey the flavour of some of the difficulties that can occur:

"We can't afford any more time overruns on export contracts; we could be out of business in two years."

"We thought we would need six contract programmers on the project – we ended up with thirty."

"£100,000 and we still don't have a system our administrators can use."

"Two weeks to go before client acceptance and they suddenly tell me the system's not ready."

"A design error got through into the delivered system – it's ruined our credibility with the client and it's going to blow our maintenance costs sky high."

Such problems need not be connected solely with the software aspects of a project, but it is clear that software development can be a major source of difficulty. A 1985 PACTEL study *(Benefits of Software Engineering Methods and Tools),* based on responses from 60 organisations involved in 199 projects, found that 66% of projects had overrun the timescale, 58% had met unexpected problems, 55% had exceeded budget, and 45% found the development task as difficult or complex, ie *much less than half of the projects were carried out without serious problems.*

One problem is that software can rarely, upon cursory inspection, be perceived to be faulty. Whereas the design of a physical artefact can 'advertise' obvious errors, one piece of program coding can look much like another: software testing and validation can be difficult to accomplish to the necessary standards. This means that it can be time-consuming – and therefore costly – to get the software right. A seemingly flawless piece of program may reveal unexpected faults.

Furthermore, the possibility of errors in a piece of software will increase with its *complexity* and *size.* The 'handling of complexity' – in whatever discipline – is a subject in its own right. One approach is to break down complex tasks into manageable (modular) sections, and this approach is sometimes adopted in the development of software. An increase in size does not necessarily involve an increase in complexity, though a large computer program is usually more likely to contain faults than a small one.

The failure to appreciate aspects of size and complexity is one reason why software development often runs into unexpected snags, problems with timescales, and consequent expenditure that runs beyond allocated budgets. A project that runs late may incur costs that are disproportionately higher than the actual extra development time that is required: the purchaser may have insisted on contractual penalty clauses, in-house staff may be taken off other important commercial work, and outside consultants may only be prepared to continue their involvement in a late project by insisting on inflated fees.

There is a further temptation, in a lengthy (or unexpectedly protracted) project, that can lead to problems. The pace of technological change, particularly in the computer industry, is such that existing purchaser commitments may quickly seem short-sighted in the light of newly emerging commercial products. How, a purchaser may ask, can the current software development be adapted to accommodate improved hardware? How are newly perceived re-quirements to be met? There is the danger in such circumstances of unrealistically prolonging software development – to the point where deadlines are not met, and budgets are hopelessly adrift.

Even where no attempt is made to accommodate technolgical innovation, the results of software de-velopment may be tardy or unsuited to the intended applications. There then follow post mortems, re-criminations, law suits and other events unlikely to impress purchasers with the delights of computerisa-tion. Perhaps the intending user failed to define the requirements in sufficient detail. Perhaps the system developers failed to follow well-defined specifica-tions. Perhaps no-one involved in the project was well-versed in the methods and techniques that could help to bring the development task to a successful conclusion.

There is thus a clear need for the task of software development to be approached in a systematic way. The various problems that may occur – relating to deadlines, costs, program reliability, etc – can be made less likely if software development is tackled in full knowledge of the attitudes, methods and tools that are available. It is the purpose of software engineering to help to ensure that the critical task of software development is approached in such a way.

Before looking at the nature and impact of software engineering in more detail, it is worth glancing at *software* and *engineering* as entities that have, until recently, evolved in parallel. We can ask: what is software? and what is engineering?

WHAT IS SOFTWARE?

The nature of software (and engineering) has to be appreciated before the flavour of software engineering can be appreciated. Modern computer software is a unique phenomenon. In earlier times there were sequences of coded instructions – effective programs – to allow particular tasks (weaving, music generation, etc) to be performed. But the complex interaction between detailed artificial languages and digital electronic equipment is a phenomenon of only the last four decades.

It is worth emphasising two aspects of modern software:

— there are many types of software, structured and coded for many different types of purpose;

— software is essentially an abstract, logical or symbolic product (or range of products). The software artefact is different in important ways from the vast range of other products produced by conventional engineering techniques.

In one familiar breakdown, software is divided into two broad classes. *Systems* software is intended to service other types of software (for example, *applications* software). Typical systems software includes: compilers, editors, file management utilities, operating system facilities and telecommunication processors. Systems software interacts with computer hardware at many levels, and it usually involves concurrent operation that requires scheduling, the sharing of resources and effective process management.

Applications software is intended to perform the specific ('real-world') tasks that the user requires. For example, business information processing is the largest single software application sector. Here a wide range of software systems − payroll, accounts receivable/payable, inventory, sales forecasting, etc − is available, with other software systems available in other applications sectors (such as industrial engineering, scientific research, education and communications). In some instances, discrete software systems have converged to provide integrated management information systems (MIS) that have access to large databases holding comprehensive business information. Increasingly there are efforts to market applications software that 'contains artificial intelligence', a recent development intended to aid human decision making in various subject areas. It is also important to appreciate the sheer size of modern software systems: a typical product may contain many times more information than the average novel − and every detail in every coded line of program needs to be correct.

Software is written in artificial programming languages appropriate to particular disciplines and applications. Each programming language has its own vocabulary, syntax and semantics; and can be translated into a language version (machine-level language) that the computer hardware can interpret in order to perform the required operations. A piece of software may embody an *algorithm,* a well-formed mathematical expression for the execution of a task; or other devices may be employed (for example, *heuristic* procedures, akin to 'rule of thumb', that do not embody an exhaustive definition of all procedural options).

We have also emphasised that software is an abstract, rather than a physical, entity. This distinguishes it from most other engineered products. Software, once designed, has no manufacturing phase, though it does need to be maintained: software does not deteriorate (ie wear out) in use – but flaws may be discovered when it runs, and changing application requirements may make software modifications essential.

WHAT IS ENGINEERING?

Engineering, traditionally viewed, is about using knowledge of natural principles (scientific law, the properties of matter, etc) to design and build artefacts. In engineering the intention is to marry theory and practice to yield effective real-life products that can serve a preconceived purpose.

One dictionary sees the term *engineer* as 'a wide one', but one 'properly confined to one qualified to design and supervise the execution of mechanical, electrical, hydraulic, and other devices, public works, etc.' Elsewhere an engineer is 'one who designs or makes, or puts to practical use, engines or machinery of any type, including electrical: one who designs or constructs public works, such as roads, railways, sewers, bridges, harbours, canals, etc: one who constructs or manages military fortifications, etc.'

It is obvious that the engineer uses rules and principles to achieve design and manufacturing objectives: use is made of formalised methods which, in the modern world, are increasingly automated. Today's engineer expects to employ a wide range of computer-based techniques to allow graphics simulations, modelling, prototyping and other design aids.

We may conclude, partly by way of summary, that the conventional engineer:

— has an understanding of natural principles;

— uses this understanding to design physical artefacts to meet preconceived practical requirements;

— exploits formalised (often automated) methods to aid the design task.

Now we can see how the conventional engineering approach can be applied to the development of computer software.

WHAT IS SOFTWARE ENGINEERING?

An initial point of interest is that the term *software engineering* is not new: it dates back to the 1950s.

Three decades ago it was first perceived that software could be 'engineered' to produce the best results. Such a view was expressed in the literature, and seminars were held in the 1960s and 1970s to explore the virtues of software engineering. For example, one conference, sponsored by the Nato Science Committee and held in Rome in October 1969, was called 'Software Engineering Techniques' (a report was published in April 1970). Another book, *Software Engineering,* was based on the Proceedings of the Third Symposium on Computer and Information Sciences, held in Florida in December 1969 (publication in 1971). Since software engineering is now 'flavour of the month' it is interesting to remember that, like artificial intelligence, it has a venerable history.

Early attitudes to software engineering were somewhat promiscuous, ie poorly organised, without an overall unifying integration. Almost any activity that related to program development could be deemed an aspect of software engineering: compiler writing, program portability, software validation, linguistic analysis, syntax design, etc – all could be drafted to play a part in software engineering. Debates were conducted to explore the possible differences between software engineering and the software elements of computer science. Were there indeed any differences? What was their nature?

The new interest in software engineering has been stimulated by the emergence of 'fourth generation' tools designed to aid the task of software development (see The Relevance of Automation, below). It is hoped that the new facilities will help in the generation of effective software within deadlines and within budgets. In these circumstances we can explore what is now being meant by 'software engineering'.

In *Webster's New Intercollegiate Dictionary* (1979), 'software' is seen as 'the entire set of programs, procedures and related documentation associated with a system and especially a computer system'; with 'engineering' defined as 'the application of science and mathematics by which the properties of matter and the sources of energy in nature are made useful to man in structures, machines, products, systems, and processes' (note how this definition implies that engineered artefacts need not be physical).

These two definitions are then combined to produce a definition of *software engineering:*

'...the application of science and mathematics by which the capabilities of computer equipment are made useful to man via computer programs, procedures, and associated documentation.'

There is an implication here that software engineering deals with more than simple programs. It has been suggested, for example, that the competent software engineer should be able to produce adequate databases, good documentation, and operational procedures for computer systems. And it is also essential that the software engineer develop software in a way that is most useful for the human operators: it is not enough just to code the requirements specifications – there is also a social dimension to software engineering. This also implies budgetary and deadline constraints. The most elegant and effective software may be useless if it is late and too costly.

There is a view that software engineering is simply 'engineering with software poured into it', ie that the basic engineering philosophy is independent of the subject matter. To engineer software, it is argued, is much the same as to engineer any other product. So anything built for a purpose requires the engineer to define the purpose, design a solution, build the product, and test the product against its purpose. This is true whatever the engineering environment: mechanical, chemical, electrical, civil, etc – and it applies equally to the development of software.

At the same time it is worth indicating how software engineering differs from other sorts of engineering. We have already noted the absence of a manufacturing phase in the development of software. With traditional engineering, design activity is followed by actual fabrication: a physical artefact is manufactured out of selected materials. There is nothing analogous in software engineering. Here, when design is complete, the product is available. It will need to be maintained but is unconstrained by physical problems: a piece of software does not corrode, wear or suffer from metal fatigue.

This means that software engineering is closely analogous to other types of engineering, but not identical. The phases involved in the generation of a physical product cannot be 'mapped onto' the development of a piece of software. Indeed software has its own characteristic 'life cycle' (see Aspects of the Life Cycle, below). Thus it can be helpful to interpret software engineering in traditional engineering terms but the analogy should not be adopted slavishly. In an Open University publication on software engineering (*What is Software Engineering?*, 1985) it is pointed out that: 'Unlike other types of engineering, the inputs and outputs of the various stages are not material objects, or even descriptions of material objects. They are descriptions of behaviour (eventually programs) or abstract structures (eventually data) expressed in a wide variety of notations.'

In another account (Ould and Southwell, 1984), it is suggested that the key elements of an engineering discipline are project management (who and when), engineering techniques (how), and tools (what with). It is easy to see how these elements (considered below) are applicable to the task of software engineering. Dp staff may be advised to act 'more like engineers' (Jones, 1986), and this is obviously sound advice where it is intended to focus on such requirements as the best use of tools and techniques.

The essence of software engineering is the development and use of systematic strategies for the production of software that:

— meets application requirements;

— exploits existing methods and tools;

— is available on time;

— is available within budget;

— allows for easy maintenance and support.

The important consideration is that, as far as possible, trouble-free software be developed by means of an optimum use of resources. Achieving this task is more important than what we call it.

ASPECTS OF THE LIFE CYCLE

It is important for managers to be able to control the various stages in software development. To a large extent it is sufficient to follow the well tried practices of project management. For example, the steps shown in Figure 1.1 are traced in a typical product-

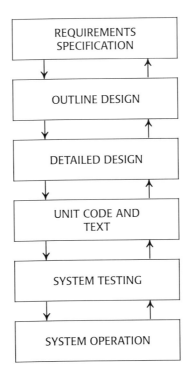

Figure 1.1

development procedure. This is an unremarkable sequence of operations, and it will be familiar to project managers in many different fields. It does however lay emphasis on the need to proceed in an orderly fashion, the need for each step to meet the specifications of the previous one, the need to meet the overall defined requirement, and the need (where appropriate) to rework a previous stage in the light of later work. The typical product-development procedure is a 'bare bones' sequence that can be adapted for the engineering of software products.

Use can also be made of two process concepts that are familiar in other areas of product development: with *incremental delivery,* the process is divided into parts and results are delivered in a staged fashion; with *prototyping,* economic working models of particular systems features are produced. The simple model can be developed to show the activity chart of Figure 1.2.

Again the activity chart shows that management should break down the overall development programme into clearly defined steps. The time needed for each activity should be carefully estimated and related to the other steps in the sequence. Each step should be defined in such a way that its completion produces a clear result. Finally there should be a smooth progression through the various steps from the initial analysis of requirements to the effective operation of the system. Such considerations are common in project management and can be applied with profit to the task of software development.

The various steps in the software development sequence are referred to as the *life cycle* – which may

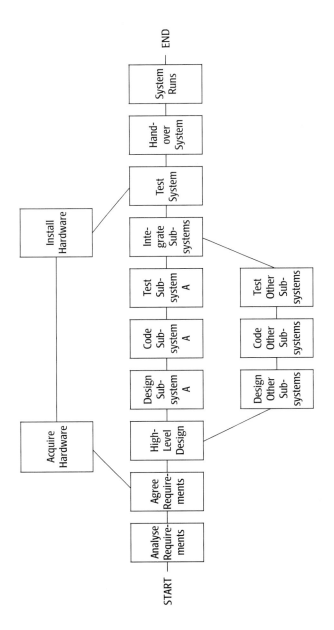

Figure 1.2   Project Development Activity Network

be regarded as a project management sequence adapted to the specific needs of software production. In fact there are many different life cycles described in the literature, varying according to the degree of detail being considered and the prevailing philosophy used to interpret the development task. The simplest life cycle model can easily be related to the more complex versions. In the simplest model (compare with Figure 1.2) the various linked steps in the development life cycle are:

—   *Requirements analysis,* involving an exploration of the user's specific needs (What problems are to be solved? What is the system expected to achieve?);

—   *Requirements specification,* where a detailed definition is given of the identified user requirements;

—   *Systems design,* where a description is provided of how the software is to meet the needs of the requirements specification;

—   *Software implementation,* where the programs are written for the systems design;

—   *Software testing* (or validation) where the quality of the software is assessed to ensure that it performs as intended;

—   *Software release,* where the completed systems are made available to the user for the intended application;

— *Software maintenance,* where the software has to be modified when errors are detected or new requirements emerge.

These development phases are shown in Figure 1.3. This is a very simplified representation. For instance, validation can take place at all stages of the life cycle, and validation that follows the implementation stage can reveal errors that occurred during earlier phases of the life cycle (eg during requirements specification). It is costly to correct errors that occurred at an early stage of the life cycle, once the software has been implemented, because all the subsequent steps have to be repeated (requirements have to be specified anew, and fresh design and implementation activities have to be undertaken).

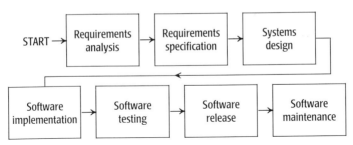

Figure 1.3
Simple Software Development Life Cycle Model

The importance of the life cycle is that the task of software development is broken down into manageable steps: when each is complete, a baseline is established for the initiation of the next phase. The aim of this systematic approach, ie the raison d'être of software engineering, is to facilitate the development of good quality software within timescales and budgets.

THE RELEVANCE OF AUTOMATION

General

Automation is concerned with the design, implementation and operation of systems that need little or no human intervention. In principle, it is possible to automate any type of labour-intensive process, though the degree of automation – at least in the initial stages – will depend upon the character of the task. It is easiest to automate simple mechanical processes (mechanisation was the precursor to modern automation); hardest to automate human activities that require commonsense, creative ability, judgement, or initiative in unprecedented situations.

Modern automation – for example, in chemical process control and factory production – is usually supervised by computer (we should remember that the early mechanisation associated with Henry Ford and other industrialists achieved great successes in the pre-computer age). Today we are seeing how computer-based methods can be introduced into the software professions themselves. Just as engineering concepts are becoming increasingly relevant to software development, so automation is helping 'software engineers' to achieve their objectives. It is now possible to automate much of the software developer's work, much in the way that computer-based systems have brought automation into the working lives of others. As with automation in other areas, it is hoped that automation of software development will bring the benefits of speed, economy and effectiveness in the generation of high-quality products.

Tools, Aids and Methods

The tools and methods used in software engineering are themselves pieces of software – developed in-house or obtained as proprietary products for particular purposes. For many years it has been conventional for software developers to use computers in their work. Today this practice is being radically extended by the provision of software tools and methods that can assist with every stage of the software-development life cycle.

The software tools can be used to support most of the technical activities involved in developing software systems. They can assist with every stage – from requirements analysis, through systems design and implementation, to testing the various systems components and eventually the overall system. They help in the whole process of designing and building a software system to budget and on time.

Software tools, like software engineering, are not a new idea: some were in use thirty years ago. The early systems, however, were limited in scope and flexibility, and in the areas to which they could be applied. Today software tools are often powerful 'new-generation' systems, available to automate many of the tasks involved in software development. They can also help users to comprehend and control large development projects. At the same time it is essential that staff be trained to use the right tools for the right jobs. As in other forms of engineering, the wrong use of a powerful tool can bring disaster.

FOURTH-GENERATION SYSTEMS

In one categorisation the first and second generations of software involved the use of machine code and assembler. COBOL and other high-level languages first appeared more than thirty years ago, and have been depicted as third-generation facilities. Today a range of fourth-generation techniques is rapidly emerging, many of which have direct relevance to software engineering.

There are now fourth-generation languages, application generators, modular software designs with reusable components, and special tools for product specification, quality control, systems design, etc. A fourth-generation system (4GS) has been defined as an integrated set of software engineering tools, which has evolved to provide an environment for the support of the production and development of interactive transaction processing applications and for ad hoc access to an applications database. Various key characteristics of 4GS can be identified:

— interactive use via terminals and workstations;

— support for multi-user access;

— rapid response to queries;

— applications generation capability;

— use of a data dictionary and a database;

— high-level end-user facilities (possibly interfacing to COBOL or FORTRAN);

— free format and conversational features.

Fourth-generation systems that 'contain AI' are now available. Some of these, using knowledge-based techniques, can serve as intelligent tools in the development of software systems.

AIMS OF SOFTWARE ENGINEERING

It is worth indicating, partly as summary, the central aims of software engineering. The methodology is based on the established techniques, methods and controls that have evolved in hardware development. There are differences between hardware and software engineering (for example, the absence in software of critical 'stuff' out of which the product is fabricated), but also substantial similarities that allow a common approach to such aspects as planning, development and management control. In particular, software engineering:

— aims to develop a well-defined methodology that can be applied to the software-development life cycle;

— seeks software components that can document the various stages in the life cycle;

— seeks to define 'milestones' that can be reviewed in a systematic way during the task of software development.

In this way it is hoped that software engineering will achieve higher reliability, cheaper maintenance costs, documentation in consistent format, visibility of progress, early detection/correction of errors, more accurate estimating, and better control of costs and timescales.

2 The Need for Software Engineering

INTRODUCTION

It is well known that, whereas computer hardware is relatively cheap and easily available, software can be expensive to develop and not always ideally suited to a user's needs. The most advanced hardware designs are not far from the limits that will be imposed by the laws of physics – which is one reason why alternative hardware architectures (data flow, parallel processing, etc) are being explored. By contrast, software design is only constrained by the limits of human ingenuity (perhaps also subject to the laws of physics). In short, hardware is a well-defined known quantity whereas software is more problematic. This circumstance has resource implications for businessmen, managers and others seeking to implement effective computer applications.

We have seen that software engineering is intended to assist the development of good-quality software within budgets and timescales. A central aim is to overcome what has been called the 'software crisis' (see below), where the requirement for applications software is not being adequately met because of the shortage of specialist staff. This chapter considers aspects of the software crisis (costs, shortage of specialists, etc), and emphasises the contribution that software engineering is intended to make in this critical situation.

THE SOFTWARE SCENE

The software scene is highly complex. Computer users can develop their own systems or use external firms who can provide off-the-shelf products or build systems from scratch to meet the user's requirements (in the UK, for example, there are in excess of 2000 software houses providing products for a growing spectrum of computer users). The rapid growth of the user population has made great demands on software vendors and others interested in supplying software products. Vendors have had to contend with various problems: for example, unrealistic expectations in the user community, software piracy (it has been suggested that 70% of all PC software in use could be illegal), a downturn in 1986 in the hardware market, and an evident shortage of new markets. Despite these difficulties, there are confident expectations that the overall software market will expand over the next five years. For example, the International Data Corporation expects significant market growth in the US and elsewhere (Klassen, 1986). Individual companies may expect to benefit according to how competently they exploit the potential of software engineering and other disciplines.

THE SOFTWARE CRISIS

The current software crisis has no single cause: there are various reasons why the delivery of software to users has been tardy and expensive, and why the delivered software has proved inadequate in performance. For one thing, there are a number of misconceptions in the user community. It is necessary to dispel these before software can be developed on an efficient basis.

It is sometimes assumed, for example, that where software is required it is important to begin programming at the earliest opportunity, even if the requirements have not been fully defined. The software effort can be a total failure if there are not the fullest talks between the customer and the software developer to specify all the necessary details about the application, the expected performance, design features, verification/validation aspects, etc. It may also be assumed that once the software is delivered, the developer's job is complete and he can move on to other pastures. Move on he may, but it is important to appreciate that the developed software, even after successful delivery and installation, will still need to be maintained: errors will be found, and the application requirements will change. In this sense, a piece of software can rarely, if ever, be regarded as complete. Rather it evolves in a shifting world.

It may also be assumed that reviews of progress can be kept to a minimum, or even that they are too time consuming to be carried out at all. In fact such reviews represent an essential control mechanism for the various stages of the software life cycle: as many as six distinct reviews may be required over the period of software development. The reviews may indicate that progress is unsatisfactory, that particular 'completed' subprojects do not meet requirements, or that the overall project is likely to exceed the allocated budget. Management can respond in various ways to such revelations.

One ploy is simply to add further staff to the project. This would seem an obvious tactic to ease the project back on course, but in fact it can be fraught with hazard. Additional staff will need to find out where things stand: they will need to communicate and discuss matters with the existing staff. This can cause a collapse in the development effort of the staff who have been with the project from the beginning – particularly when it is felt that new staff are being drafted to compensate for inadequate staff performance. Where management feel that additional staff should be added to a project, this should only be authorised in full knowledge of what might go wrong.

In summary, it is necessary to proceed through the software cycle in a careful systematic way, the completion of each stage establishing a realistic and secure base line for the start of the next. 'Obvious' solutions to problems may have unexpected and deleterious consequences, and as far as possible these should be anticipated. It is also important for managers to be realistic about the cost allocations at the various stages of the life cycle. For example, whereas around 10-15% of the budget is typically allocated to software maintenance, many managers have found that 50% is more realistic (Lientz and Swanson, 1980). Only when managers fully address such considerations will the worst features of the software crisis be mitigated.

It has often been suggested that a project containing a software element is likely to run into problems. Such a project 'runs a high risk of being completed late and costing significantly more than was budgeted' (Wingrove, 1986). Moreover there are also 'frequent reports that software designs do not always perform as well as they should', and the difficulties can often adversely affect the overall control of the project. Project managers may complain about poorly defined requirements, unclear specifications, ambiguous terminology, incomplete resource estimates, problems with monitoring and control, unsuitable languages and test metrics, problems with interfacing, etc. 'The list of difficulties is considerable and, overall, paints a bleak picture' (Wingrove).

Today many projects have a software content – and this is often the most problematic project component. A central problem appears to be the accurate identification and specification of requirements (What did the customer want? Were the application requirements fully understood? Clearly specified?). One estimate suggests that around 50% of the project difficulties arose because of inadequate specification of requirements and systems. It is clear that, for whatever precise reasons, software projects are often viewed with some trepidation by project managers: there is a fifty-fifty chance that any particular software project will be completed late, over budget, and with disappointing results. This indicates something of the character of the software crisis, the unsatisfactory situation that software engineering is designed to improve. Two elements that are particularly relevant to the software crisis deserve special mention: costs, and the shortage of specialists.

COSTS

Control of costs is clearly crucial to the success of a project, whether or not software development happens to be a component in the project. However, as we have seen, the difficulties that attend software development make cost control in this area particularly important. It is possible, for example, to present the life cycle model in terms of the time and effort needed to complete each phase. This information can then be used to provide realistic cost estimates. Boehm (1981) presents a hierarchy of cost-estimation models that carry the generic title COCOMO (COnstructive COst MOdel). With this approach the aim is to determine the software effort and cost as a function of the size of the software product in source instructions.

It is necessary that a software cost estimation provide a link between on the one hand the concepts and methods of economic analysis and, on the other, the characteristic elements of software engineering. Software costs – and how they relate to various development, systems and environmental factors – need to be estimated in order that the typical commercial calculations (for cost-benefit, make-or-buy, etc) can be undertaken. In this way, the software element of a project is a typical component for which financial resources have to be allocated, and it needs to be assessed in normal commercial terms. Without a realistic estimate of costs, software developers are in no position to tell a manager or client that the budgets and/or schedules are impractical – they become 'locked in' to an impossible timescale that can only end in disaster. In a worst-case scenario the project is totally out-of-control from the start.

One estimate suggests that by 1980 the cost of software in the US was around 40 billion dollars, 2% of the Gross National Product; and software costs are continuing to expand faster than the economy in general. The disparate trends in computer hardware and software are such that it is increasingly realistic to regard the hardware as packaging for software that largely determines the values of the overall system. Seventy or eighty per cent of the cost of a typical system may be spent on software, with software increasingly regarded as the main element in an industry achieving around 10% of US Gross National Product. In such circumstances the need for effective software engineering is obvious.

With software development such a dominant element in a typical computer system project, software costs are high enough, even in a well-planned project. In a badly-planned project – for example, when important software errors are detected late in the life cycle – startling cost penalties can emerge (in some cases, factors of 100 are involved!). When this is appreciated by project managers and senior executives, it is easy to see that systematic software engineering is an essential element in projects that include software development. One estimate (PA Computers and Telecommunications, 1985) suggests that the use of automated tools, an important component of software engineering, could bring considerable benefits to UK industry:

— £260 million savings from the use of improved management tools;

— £100 million from the use of specification, design and generation tools.

The £360 million total per annum is reckoned to be equivalent in cost terms to the employment of around 24,000 software engineering staff. Similarly a reduction from 20% to 15% of the software engineers engaged on maintenance and enhancement, achieved through the increased use of automated tools, would indicate benefits of around £57 million, the equivalent of 4000 software engineering staff.

Thus software engineering is intended to bring identifiable cost benefits to project management where software development is an important project component. The provision of automated methods is seen as a cost-effective approach to a wide range of software development needs, both on account of the current costs of software staff and the functional efficiency of the automated provisions. Staff costs are related in part to the current shortage of specialists, another key factor in the software crisis.

SHORTAGE OF SPECIALISTS

There are various estimates of the number of staff, in the UK and elsewhere, involved in software engineering. For example, the PA Computers and Telecommunications (PACTEL) study (1985) suggests that by 1983 there were about 82,000 software engineers employed in the UK, with a significant increase (to 84,000) anticipated for 1985.

At the same time, in the UK and abroad, there is a perceived shortage of software specialists. According to the UK Institution of Electrical Engineers (IEE), there is an annual shortage of 1500 graduates in the new software technologies. (Similarly the Engineering Industry Training Board estimates that the 3000 technicians trained each year are half the number needed.) To help overcome the shortage of software specialists, the NCC and the IEE are aiming to introduce a national certificate in software engineering in September 1987. The Alvey Directorate has estimated that the current shortage of software engineers is likely to reach 5000 by 1988, if appropriate steps are not taken.

The increasing availability of software engineering methods and tools − in particular, the provision of automated facilities − will help to offset the shortage of specialists in the years ahead. However, it is important to keep this situation in perspective. We have seen that software engineering is not a magic cure-all; nor are the automated tools and methods by which it is characterised. Staff will need to be trained to use the new techniques, and software engineering should not be regarded solely as a means of overcoming specialist shortages. It can help, to a degree, in this situation, but software engineering should be implemented as a systematic approach to the development of good-quality software within budgets and timescales.

Appendix 1

Where to Go for Help

Where to Go for Help

There are various groups and initiatives (some supported by NEDO and DTI) that provide information on software tools and methods (and on other aspects of software engineering). Particular attention should be given to:

STARTS: NCC Ltd, 11 New Fetter Lane, London EC4A 1PU. STARTS − Software Tools for Application to large Real-Time Systems − has produced the STARTS handbook, currently being revised. This is a definitive guide to software tools and methods for use in large systems.

A series of 10 debrief reports has been published on individual tools and methods written by practical experts:

SLIM (a project estimating tool)
PRICE S (a project estimating tool)
ARTEMIS (a project management tool)

VDM (Vienna Development Method. A rigorous mathematical method for top level specification and design of data-dominated applications)

SOFCHIP (a method based on asynchronous architecture and covering the whole life cycle)

JSD (Jackson System Development)

SDL (System Design Language)

SAFRA (a suite of tools using CORE, MASCOT, PERSPECTIVE and supporting PASCAL)

CORE (a method for expressing requirements)

Z (a rigorous system specification technique)

(Each report costs £10.00; postage and packing — under £20 – £2.30, over £20 – £4.60. Orders, with remittance, to SALES ADMINISTRATION, NCC Ltd, Oxford Road, Manchester M1 7ED)

The STARTS Purchasers' Handbook – This STARTS publication is produced by the Public Purchaser Group of seven major users of large real-time systems. It outlines the best practice in specifying and purchasing real-time systems, and indicates the level of software engineering that the purchasers will expect from their suppliers by giving examples of sets of methods and tools and guidance for compliance. The Handbook includes an overview, checklists, appendices and bibliography.

(The STARTS Purchasers' Handbook costs £9.50. Orders, with remittance, to SALES ADMINISTRATION, NCC Ltd, Oxford Road, Manchester M1 7ED)

STDC – the Software Tools Demonstration Centre – has installed a representative collection of software tools covering all technical aspects of software development, and the management of software projects. Demonstrations of these tools are given by appointment to small groups of two or three people at the purpose-designed centre in Manchester. (NCC Ltd, Oxford Road, Manchester M1 7ED)

STDC also operates an enquiry service about software tools and methods in conjunction with the STARTS initiative. Details of more than 200 products are included in the information base.

STDC publishes a newsletter "Software Engineering Tools and Methods" six times a year, and various reports and guides. It also runs seminars, courses and workshops.

The Alvey Directorate is active in software engineering, with many developments in progress in different institutions and organisations.

The Directorate publishes a newsletter, and has various special interest groups and clubs which meet regularly.

Full details from: Software Engineering, The Alvey Directorate, Millbank Tower, Millbank, London SW1P 4QU.

Appendix 2

Glossary

Glossary

Application

The user task performed by a computer (such as making a hotel reservation, processing a company's accounts or analysing market-research data).

Applications software

The software used to carry out the applications task.

Artificial intelligence (AI)

Applications that would appear to show intelligence if they were carried out by a human being. Mimicry or duplication, by computers, of mental activities.

Automation

Systems that can operate with little or no human intervention. It is easiest to automate simple mechanical processes; hardest to automate those tasks needing

	commonsense, creative ability, judgement, or initiative in unprecedented situations.
Data	Usually the same as information. Sometimes information is regarded as processed data.
Data design	The design of the data structure needed by a particular software system.
Data preparation	The conversion of data (perhaps collected manually) to make it suitable for subsequent computer input.
Engineer	A person who uses knowledge of science and mathematics to design and implement machinery and systems that operate in the world (see also Software engineering).
Engineering	The activities of the engineer.
Fifth-generation systems	Computer systems being researched and designed to embody artificial intelligence.
Fourth-generation systems	Computer systems, available and being developed, to introduce higher levels of automation into a range of processes, including the production of software.

Functional specification	The definition of a piece of software in terms of the functions it is intended to perform.
Hardware	The physical equipment in a computer system. It is usually contrasted with software.
Implementation	The process of converting the notation used to express detailed software design into the program code (also known as coding or programming). Implementation also denotes the task of bringing together the various systems components to get the system working (also known as commissioning).
Life cycle	The sequence of stages or phases, from requirements analysis to maintenance, involved in software development.
Maintenance	The task of modifying (correcting, updating, etc) a software system after it has been put into operation.
Methods	The software-supported approach to achieving the various phases of the life cycle. Methods are usually regarded as functionally similar to tools.

Modelling	Simulation of a system by manipulating a number of interactive variables; can answer 'what if…?' questions to predict the behaviour of the modelled system. A model of a system or subsystem is often called a prototype.
Modularisation	The splitting up of a software system into a number of manageable sections (modules) to ease design, coding, etc.
Project management	The systematic approach for analysing, organising and completing a project, of whatever type.
Prototype	see Modelling.
Requirements analysis	The analysis of a user's needs and the conversion of these into a statement of requirements, prior to specification.
Software	The collection of programs intended to cause computer hardware to function in particular ways.
Software development life cycle	see Life cycle.
Software engineering	The development and use of systematic strategies (themselves often software based) for the

production of good-quality soft-ware within budgets and time-scales.

Systems design   The process of establishing the overall architecture of a software system.

Systems
software   Software, such as an operating system, concerned mainly with 'house-keeping' tasks, managing the hardware resources, etc. It is usually contrasted with applica-tions software.

Testing   The process of executing software with test data to check that it satis-fies the specification. Testing is a major part of validation.

Tools   Aids (usually software based) to achieving the various phases of the software development life cycle. Tools are usually regarded as functionally similar to methods.

Validation   The process of checking a specific piece of life-cycle notation, and the conversion from one piece of nota-tion to another (see also Testing).

Verification   The process of proving that a program meets its specification.

Appendix 3

References and Bibliography

References and Bibliography

Abbott R J, *Software Development,* John Wiley, 1986.

Basili V R, Selby R W and Hutchens D H, Experimentation in software engineering, *IEEE Transactions on Software Engineering,* July 1986, pp 733-743.

Basili V R and Weiss D M, A methodology for collecting valid software and engineering data, *IEEE Transactions on Software Engineering,* November 1984, pp 728-737.

Beregi W E, Architecture prototyping in the software engineering environment, *IBM Systems Journal,* Vol. 23, No. 1, 1984, pp 4-35.

Boehm B W, *Software Engineering Economics,* Prentice-Hall Inc., Englewood Cliffs, New Jersey 07632, 1981.

Born G, Controlling software quality, *Software Engineering Journal*, January 1986, pp 24-28.

Brown P, Managing software development, *Datamation*, 15 April 1985, pp 133-136.

Carrotte G, Measures of productivity, *Data Processing*, September 1984, pp 20-22.

Developing high-quality systems faster, *EDP Analyzer*, June 1986, pp 1-11.

Duncan M, Revival of the fittest: new vigor for your development life cycle, *Computerworld*, 2 June 1986, pp 79-84.

Gomaa H, A software design method for real-time systems, *Communications of the ACM*, September 1984, pp 938-949.

Hecht H and Hecht M, Software reliability in the system context, *IEEE Transactions on Software Engineering*, January 1986, pp 51-58.

Huff K E, Sroka J V and Struble D D, Quantitative models for managing software development processes, *Software Engineering Journal*, January 1986, pp 17-23.

Jeffery D R and Lawrence M J, Managing programming productivity, *Journal of Systems and Software*, 5, 1985, pp 49-58.

Jones R, Engineering the best possible dp solution?, *Computing*, 19 June 1986, p 26.

Klassen R H, The changing world of software markets, *Canadian Datasystems,* June 1986, pp 56-60.

Lantz K, The prototyping methodology: designing right the first time, *Computerworld,* 7 April 1986, pp 69-72.

Laughery K R Jr. and Laughery K R Sr., Human factors in software engineering: a review of the literature, *Journal of Systems and Software,* 5, 1985, pp 3-14.

Lientz B and Swanson E, *Software Maintenance Management,* Addison-Wesley, 1980.

Mathis R F, The last 10 percent, *IEEE Transactions on Software Engineering,* June 1986, pp 705-712.

Mellor P, Field monitoring of software maintenance, *Software Engineering Journal,* January 1986, pp 43-49.

Omotayo O R, Designing user-friendly software systems, *Data Processing,* June 1984, pp 16-18.

Ould M and Southwell K, *Software Engineering,* NCC, 1984.

PA Computers and Telecommunications (PACTEL), for the Department of Trade and Industry, *Benefits of Software Engineering Methods and Tools,* June 1985.

Pressman R S, *Software Engineering: A Practitioner's Approach,* McGraw-Hill, 1982.

Pruijm R A M, The audit of software maintenance, *EDPACS,* August 1986, pp 1-5.

Ringland G, Software engineering in a development group, *Software – Practice and Experience,* June 1984, pp 533-559.

Rook P, Controlling software projects, *Software Engineering Journal,* January 1986, pp 7-16.

Software Engineering Techniques, Report on a conference sponsored by the NATO Science Committee, Rome, Italy, 27-31 October 1969.

Speeding up application development, *EDP Analyzer,* April 1985, pp 1-12.

STARTS Public Purchaser Group, with the support of the DTI and NCC, *The STARTS Purchasers' Handbook,* 1986.

Thadhani A J, Factors affecting programmer productivity during application development, *IBM Systems Journal,* Vol. 23, No. 1, 1984, pp 19-35.

The STARTS Guide, prepared by the industry with the support of the DTI, NEDO and NCC, 1984.

The system development spectrum, *EDP Analyzer,* April 1986, pp 1-11.

Tou J T (ed), *Software Engineering,* Vol. 1 and 2, Academic Press, 1971.

Tucker M, Tools speed software integration, *Mini-Micro Systems,* February 1986, pp 55-63.

Weber H, Specification of modular systems, *IEEE Transactions on Software Engineering,* July 1986, pp 784-797.

Wingrove A, The problems of managing software projects, *Software Engineering Journal,* January 1986, pp 3-6.

Zvegintzov N, Software maintenance: building tomorrow on today, *Data Management,* March 1984, pp 33-40.